COLONIAL AMERICAN ★ ★ ★ CRAFTS ★ ★ ★
The School

Catchpenny prints. Popular 18th century printed sheets of paper filled with illustrations and a verse. They were sold on the streets for a penny. Later on they were stitched together to form chapbooks. These chapbooks were a form of early children's books.

COLONIAL AMERICAN ★ ★ ★ CRAFTS ★ ★ ★

The School

By Judith Hoffman Corwin

FRANKLIN WATTS
New York/London/Toronto/Sydney/1989

For Virginia Dare,
the first child born of settlers
in this brave new land
(August 18, 1587),
and all the others that followed,
especially, my son, Oliver Jamie.

Library of Congress Cataloging-in-Publication Data

Corwin, Judith Hoffman.
    Colonial American crafts : the school / by Judith Hoffman Corwin.
      p.   cm.
    Includes index.
    Summary: A collection of recipes and instructions for other
projects relating to life in colonial America, particularly activities that
might have taken place in the schools.
    ISBN 0-531-10714-0
    1. Handicraft—United States—Juvenile literature. 2. Cookery,
American—Juvenile literature. 3. United States—Social life and
customs—Colonial period, ca. 1600–1775—Juvenile literature.
[1. Handicraft. 2. Cookery, American. 3. United States—Social life
and customs—Colonial period, ca. 1600–1775.] I. Title. II. Title:
Colonial American crafts. School.
TT23.C662   1989
745.5—dc20   89-32542 CIP AC

Contents

Battledore (18th century printed book) with alphabet and pictures

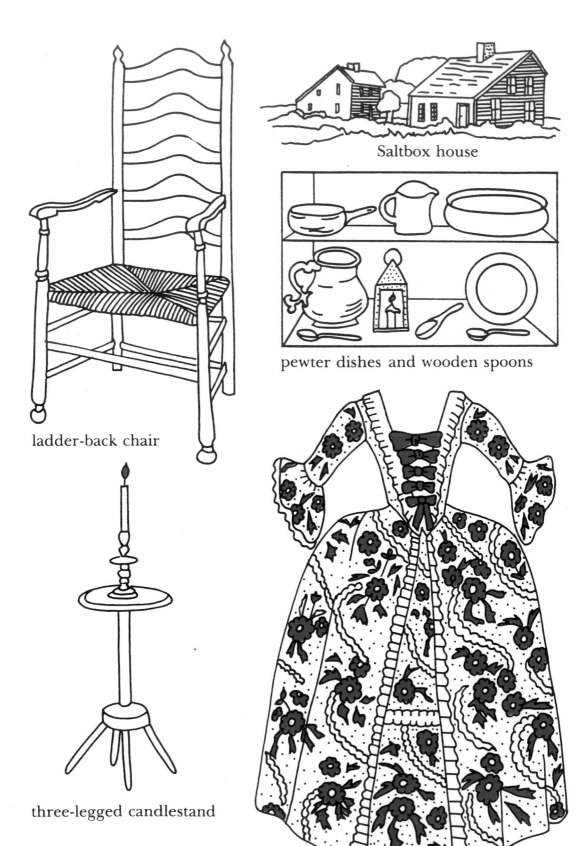

ladder-back chair

Saltbox house

pewter dishes and wooden spoons

three-legged candlestand

1700s American dress

6

About This Book ★

This book deals with the colonial period in America, from about 1607 to 1776, just before the signing of the Declaration of Independence. During this time, the colonists were settling into their new environment and were establishing a new life for themselves. We will discover that everyday things—houses, furniture, clothes, tools, food, toys, dishes, candlesticks, and even nails—can all express the character of the time in which the colonists lived.

The first European immigrants to the vast untamed coast of America came to Plymouth, Massachusetts; to New Netherland (which is now New York state); to the Middle Colonies such as New Jersey, Pennsylvania, Maryland, and Delaware; to North and South Carolina; and to Virginia. These first settlers braved the challenge of survival in an unknown land thousands of miles from familiar surroundings, family, and friends. They came for many different reasons, such as the possibility of a brand-new way of life that offered religious freedom, a chance to own their own land, or the promise of a better future.

The colonists came from many countries—England, France, Holland, Germany, and Spain. They brought with them their different customs and skills. There was an exchange of cultures between these settlers and the first Americans—the Indians. The combining of these cultures and the cleverness of using the materials that were found in the "New World" resulted in a new and exciting way of life.

The living conditions were simpler then, and the general knowledge of the first settlers was less extensive than it is today. Daily life was similar to what it would be like for us on a camping trip. Life depended on the weather and on the seasons. The early settlers had only the bare necessities of life.

The colonists found it very hard work to survive in this strange, new land. If they were lucky enough to live through the rough sea voyage, many died during their first years here. They relied on the friendly Indians for help in learning how to grow new foods like corn, cranberries, pumpkins, and squash and where to hunt and fish. The settlers built homes for themselves and their families. At first, some dug caves in the hills or built tipis like the ones the Indians lived in. Other early structures were made from logs with sailcloth stretched over them and raised stockades.

Eventually, the people were able to build and develop towns with wood frame, stone, and brick houses; a mill; a blacksmith's shop; taverns; a schoolhouse; a bakery; a print shop; a lacemakers' shop; a music shop; a general store; a church; a meetinghouse; and even a wigmaker's shop. By the year 1733, there were thirteen colonies. The men and women had to know how to plant and harvest crops, tend to livestock, cook and preserve their own food, make candles, weave cloth, make their own clothes, shear sheep, cure ills, forecast weather, and even embroider and sew patchwork quilts. Children worked hard alongside their parents in order for their family to survive and eventually prosper.

When America was young, almost everything people needed was handmade. The colonists took great pride in the things that they made for everyday use. These everyday items were functional, and many were beautifully crafted. Early American colonists gave us a heritage rich in charming customs and wonderful arts and crafts. We can learn from what they were able to develop and make use of.

Honesty, hard work, a sensible nature, and the ability to work together to solve their problems enabled the colonists to survive in a hostile environment. Try to imagine what life was like in the 1600s and 1700s in this young country. Open, unexplored, bountiful land; natural resources beyond belief; and natural beauty. No car, bus, or airplane noise. All food was grown on your land or nearby or caught in the forest.

There was no fast food, and no radio, television, or home computers. There was no electricity or gas for lighting, warmth, or cooking. Your food was cooked on the open hearth in the middle of the kitchen. Your clothes were made at home by someone in your family, fashioned out of linen or wool made on your farm. You had only a few changes of clothes, and probably only one pair of shoes. Bicycles, skateboards, video games, chocolate bars, and ice cream would not be in your world.

One of the values of history is that it enables us to better understand both the people of other times and ourselves. A peek into the world of eighteenth-century America, when the nation was just beginning, is an exciting look at a trying time, but also a time of opportunity for new beginnings and a chance to be free.

There are three books in the "Colonial American Crafts" series—*The Home*, *The Village*, and *The School*. All three have participation projects that use crafts to provide insights into the lives of colonial people.

spinning wheel

grandfather clock

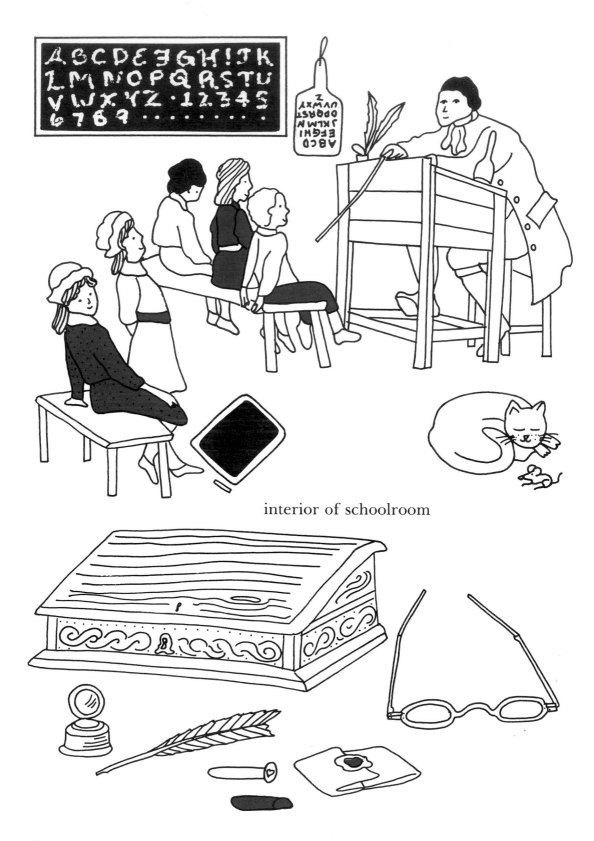

interior of schoolroom

lap desk, writing materials, sealing wax, and spectacles

The School ★

During the late colonial period, there were new ideas circulating, like the proposition that all men are created equal, and questions about the divine right of kings. But all children still didn't have the right to a free education. The idea that young people should be required to attend school at public expense was also radical, for the majority of the young people in the American colonies never even entered a schoolroom. Schools varied greatly in the American colonies.

In some, but not all, colonies, education was mandatory, but this did not mean that children actually had to go to school. The children could be taught at home; they could go to a public school; or a young person could be sent out to learn a trade and be apprenticed to a tradesman. Wealthy young people could naturally afford private or boarding schools.

Good penmanship was very important, but nobody worried very much about how words were spelled. Standard dictionaries were available, but there were often different spellings for the same word. Even teachers were judged by the quality of their penmanship.

Heavy pencils were just being introduced. They were made out of powdered graphite mixed with clay, but the most common writing tool was the quill pen, which a schoolmaster could quickly cut from a goose quill with his penknife. Good quality ink had to be imported from Europe. It came in a powdered form and had to be dissolved in vinegar in order to be used. Most students mixed their own with soot from the fire mixed with water. Rural families made their own ink by boiling down swamp-maple bark and adding sulphate to make it darker. Pupils carried their ink back and forth to school in inkhorns that were very much like powderhorns, but smaller, or in a small leather bottle.

There was no chalk or blackboards to write on, and even individual slates were few. Many children practiced their writing on birch bark with their quill pens and crude ink. Paper was very scarce and expensive; only the best private schools had white paper to write on. All other schools, if they had any paper at all, had rough paper which was dark and unruled. A stick with a string attached was used for making rules on the paper. When the large sheets of paper were doubled over twice, one sheet made four leaves, or eight pages. This could easily be made into a book when given a cover of brown wrapping paper.

Other school supplies were simple, with only a few luxuries, like a set of imported paints that had to be dissolved in water. The only visual aid available to the teacher was a globe.

hornbook

The few textbooks that could be found in the colonial classroom were bound in leather, so that they would last a long time. They were handed down from one pupil to the next. The earlier ones would probably have been printed in Europe.

Although the Bible would certainly have been included in a young person's studies, the most popular book was the New England Primer, first published before 1690 and reissued, with slight changes made, many times in the next two centuries. It introduced the alphabet with a "syllabarium," a series of syllables somewhat more difficult than the ABC hornbooks that beginners used.

What is most striking about the Primer is that it praised classroom obedience.

GOOD BOYS AT THEIR BOOKS
He who ne'er learns his A, B, C,
Forever will a Blockhead be;
But he who to his Book's inclin'd,
Will soon a Golden Treasure find.

The actual school building during colonial times would not have been built with comfort in mind. The first seats were planks set on legs. By the 1770s, most benches had backs on them. For heating, there was a large fireplace in the earlier

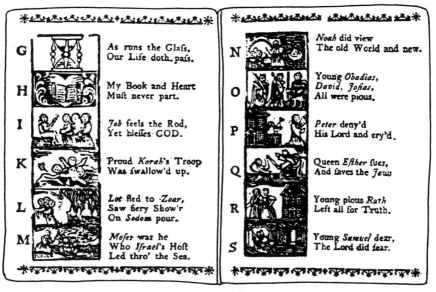

New England Primer

schools. Later on, the potbellied stove that we usually think of as being in "The Little Red Schoolhouse" was introduced.

It was hard for communities to get good teachers, and advertisements for teachers were commonly found in the local newspapers. Some of the best teachers were clergymen with college degrees. In order to inspire respect, schoolmasters began to wear a kind of uniform. This included a long, dark coat with square panels reaching down to their calves, trousers, white stockings showing underneath, buckles on their shoes, shoulder-length gray wigs, and a three-cornered hat. They could be seen carrying a cane.

Strict discipline was the order of the day. No nonsense was permitted. A dunce-cap was put on students who fooled around and they were made to sit or stand in a corner.

Teachers had a switch that they were allowed to strike their students with and even a cat-o'-nine-tails to whip the poor distracted scholar. If you were caught not paying attention to your studies, you were likely to be made to write "Idle Boy," "Tell-Tale," or other sayings many times. On the kindergarten level, in some of the dame (girl) schools, girls were mixed with the boys. But usually they only studied with the boys if it was with their own tutor at home.

In general, it was school practice to instruct girls only when the boys were not in attendance. That meant very early in the morning or perhaps late in the afternoon, or maybe in the summer when their brothers were busy working in the fields. Morning classes for the girls were held from five o'clock until seven.

Students often walked miles to attend school. Lunch was brought from home and usually consisted of a slice of bread and a piece of cheese. An apple or other piece of fruit or a cookie would have been a treat. Libraries didn't exist, so the teachers had to instruct the students with the help of a few volumes. Books were scarce, so they had to be used mostly at school and shared. Homework was usually done on a slate, written in chalk, if at all. The school year was quite short, only a few months out of the whole year.

As you have seen, the colonial period was an exciting time. The projects that follow will help to bring the colonial school alive. You will be able to share some of the experiences of those days.

schoolmaster

cut

Quill Pen

This is a super-easy pen to make! Just be careful writing with it, and don't press too hard. It will be fun to use with your homemade ink.

Here's what is needed:

a feather (6–8″ long)
a small knife (ask an adult for help in using this)

Here's how to do it:

Checking the illustration, cut each side of the tip of the feather. Try to make the sides come to a nice even point. Now you are ready to try out your new pen. Dip it in the ink and practice writing with it. You will be able to make fancy designs. Look at the illustrations at the bottom of the page for ideas. You can also make up your own designs.

Walnut Shell Ink

These are two kinds of ink that were used in the colonies. The walnut shells make a lovely brown ink, and the cranberries make a bright-red ink. Both will work beautifully with the quill pen.

Ingredients:

4 empty walnut shells, crushed
1 cup water
½ teaspoon salt
1 teaspoon vinegar

Utensils:

paper bag
hammer
small saucepan, measuring cup, cheesecloth
empty, clean jar with cover

Here's how to do it:

1. Place the walnut shells in the paper bag, and crush them with a hammer on the floor.

2. Put the crushed walnut shells into the saucepan, and add a cup of water.

3. Bring the mixture to a boil. Add the salt and vinegar. This will "set the color" of the ink. Turn down the heat and allow it to simmer for 15 minutes more.

4. Strain the ink through the cheesecloth into the jar. Put the cover on the jar and store it in a safe place until you are ready to use it.

God makes the PEN his Herald to proclaim
The splendid Glories of his Works and Name.

Abiah Holbrook

penmanship

Cranberry Ink ★

Ingredients:

1 cup fresh cranberries
2 tablespoons water

Utensils:

medium-size saucepan
measuring cup and spoons
metal spoon, metal strainer
empty, clean jar with cover

Here's how to do it:

1. Place the cranberries and water in the saucepan.

2. Bring the mixture to a boil. With the metal spoon, crush the cranberries to release their color.

3. Strain the mixture and place it in the jar. Put the cover on the jar and store in a safe place until you are ready to use it.

Paper Cuttings ★

These paper cuttings can be used as decorations or sent as greeting cards to friends. They are fun to make because with a few simple cuts, you have many images. If you like, after they have been cut out, you can decorate them with your homemade ink and quill pen.

Here's what is needed:

sheets of 8½″ × 11″ white paper, one for each paper cutting scissors, pencil

Here's how to do it:

1. To make the paper cutting, fold the paper into accordion pleats along the 11″ side. To do this you will be folding the paper into 3 equal parts. Make the first fold, then turn the paper over and make a fold on the same end, the same width as the first fold, but in the opposite direction. You will have to do this for each paper cutting.

2. Designs are given for a tree, bird, leaf, squirrel, duck, cat, and a house. Decide which one you want to make and then sketch it onto the folded paper.

3. Cut out the shape, being careful not to cut completely through the folds on either side. Unfold the paper and you will have a row of connecting designs. If you want to make longer chains, glue several chains together. You can try different designs and also glue them together to make an interesting chain.

★ ★

24

Rebecca Rag Doll

Most colonial children didn't have any store-bought toys. Their playthings were made by their parents or by themselves. Mothers sewed rag dolls from deerskin or scraps of fabric. They were stuffed with pine needles and sweet grass. You can make one doll or several. Check the illustrations for ideas.

Here's what is needed:

pencil, tracing paper, carbon paper
½ yard unbleached muslin (this should make at least four dolls and four hearts)
straight pins, scissors, needle
white sewing thread
polyester batting
black fine-line felt-tip marker
several small brushes
several colors of acrylic paint

Here's how to do it:

1. Make a pattern for the doll and the heart by tracing the designs given.

2. Fold the muslin in half. Pin the muslin so that it holds together and you can cut two pieces at a time. Place the pattern on top of the muslin and trace around the outline of it with a pencil. About ¼" away from the pattern line, cut out the pattern, leaving the pins in. Remove the pattern. This will make one doll.

26

3. Sew the two sides together on the pattern line, leaving a 1½″ opening for the stuffing to go through. Clip the curves so that the finished doll won't pucker.

4. Turn the doll inside out so the rough edges are hidden. Stuff with the batting and then stitch up the opening.

5. Draw on the doll's features, hair, and the outline of its clothes with the black marker. Then, with the acrylic paints, color them in as you like. Using the patterns given and following the same methods, you can make a stuffed heart. You can paint it and sew it to the doll's hand, as shown.

★ ★ ★ ★ ★ ★ ★ ★

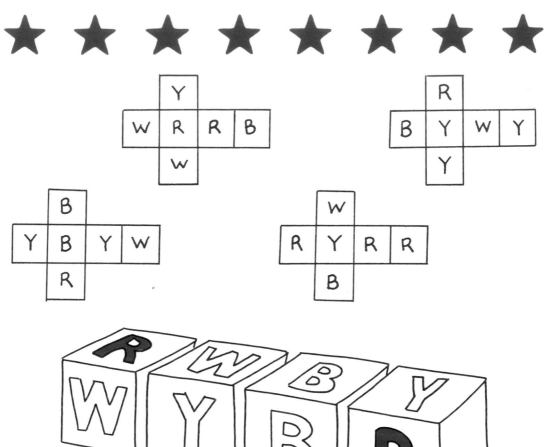

	Y		
W	R	R	B
	W		

	R		
B	Y	W	Y
	Y		

	B		
Y	B	Y	W
	R		

	W		
R	Y	R	R
	B		

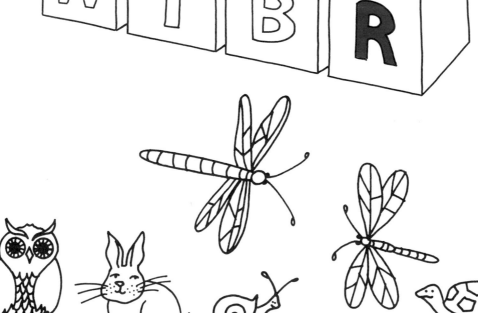

Red, White, Blue, and Yellow Puzzle

The cube puzzle is absorbing because no matter how long you work at the solution, it still seems impossible. Made from a thick white sponge and colored with felt-tipped markers, the puzzle can be great fun. The puzzle has four same-size cubes. Each face of each is colored either red, blue, or yellow. The arrangement of the colors in relation to each other on each cube is different. The object of the puzzle is to get all four cubes in a row, so that one of each of the four colors is on all four sides in a row. The colors of the end faces don't count.

Here's what is needed:

white or natural-color sponge, at least 1″ thick
pencil, ruler, scissors
red, blue, and yellow permanent felt-tip markers

Here's how to do it:

1. Measure the thickness of the sponge. With a pencil, draw a line across the sponge the same length as the thickness. Cut out four cube shapes from the sponge (all sides should be equal).

2. Using the felt-tip markers, color each of the cubes according to the four color patterns shown in the illustration. Because the sponge is white, or natural color, that side can be left alone where it is shown in the illustration.

3. You can solve the puzzle by following the illustration that shows the solution. Mix up the cubes and try to rearrange them again without looking at the solution.

4

3
4 4 4
3

4 4 4

Missing Number Trick ★

Colonial Americans had to entertain themselves and their friends. Here's a simple math trick that's fun. You are going to be able to guess what number is in the square!

Here's what is needed:

piece of paper and a pencil

Here's how to do it:

1. First ask one of your friends to draw a square and write in it any number from one to nine, without letting you see it.

2. Now tell your friend to write the same number to the right and the left of the square.

3. Ask the friend to write the number three above and below the square. Now the friend should add up all the numbers on the sheet of paper and tell you the total. When you know the total, you can tell your friend the number he or she originally wrote in the square.

4. Here's how the trick really works. First, divide your friend's total by three. Then take away two and the answer is the number in the square. In the example shown in the illustration, your friend will tell you the total is eighteen $(4 + 4 + 4 + 3 + 3)$. When you divide by three you get six $(18 \div 3)$; then six minus two equals four $(6 - 2)$.

Note: You will need to be very careful with the hammer and nails. Ask an adult to help you with this project.

Bird Feeder

There are many birds native to America that live around us— robins, thrushes, sparrows, mockingbirds, skylarks, wrens, goldfinches, and blackbirds. They would all enjoy this convenient feeder. This very simple bird feeder, when nailed to a branch of a tree or just put on a window ledge, can hold breadcrumbs or birdseed. Even if there aren't any birds around at first, be patient. As they begin to find the food, more will come every day. If you can't tell what kind of bird it is that you're feeding, you can look up information about birds in a bird-watching manual, where you will find illustrations and the names of popular birds. It will be fun to learn something about bird-watching, but you must be very still or the birds will fly away.

Here's what is needed:

scraps of wood:
    1 piece for the base of the feeder should be about 12″ square
    for the rim of the feeder you will need 4 pieces of wood
       about 6″ long
hammer and about 10 nails

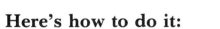

Here's how to do it:

1. You will be making a rim around the base of the feeder. This will keep the breadcrumbs from scattering all around and will give the birds something to land on.

2. Nail the four smaller boards onto the base, forming a rim around. In the center of the rim is where the breadcrumbs will go. See the illustration.

3. Now you can nail the bird feeder to a branch of a tree. Or you can just put it on a window ledge or in the garden where the birds can see it.

Old-Fashioned Christmas

The colonists enjoyed many rural festivals that were linked to the seasons. Haying and berrying parties in the summer; corn-husking and apple-picking in the fall; skating parties in the winter; and "sugaring-off" get-togethers, when the syrup was collected from the maple trees, and the gathering of salmon and shad in the spring. These were not holidays as we know them today, but just a chance for people to visit, catch up on the local gossip, and leave their daily routine behind for awhile.

In earlier colonial days religious practices of settlers, such as the Puritans, limited the festive atmosphere. But Christmas in later colonial times was celebrated by settlers cutting ever-green trees and bringing them inside to decorate with candles, popcorn and cranberry chains, paper stars, and apples. Young people enjoyed making gingerbread cookies and the warm, sweet smell of freshly baked fruit cakes perfumed the air.

Popcorn and Cranberry Chains for the Christmas Tree

These brightly colored strings helped to make the Christmas tree look festive and beautiful. The paper ornaments are also an added delight and quite simple to make. With a piece of red yarn, they can add a decorative touch that is really old-fashioned.

Here's what is needed:

long, thin needle; heavy-duty thread
scissors, small buttons
a large bag of popcorn
fresh, hard cranberries

Here's how to do it:

1. Thread a needle with the heavy-duty thread.

2. Put a large knot in one end and string a button to hold the popcorn and berries on the thread.

3. Begin to string the popcorn and the berries on the thread. You can experiment with different designs. You could try alternating popcorn and cranberries or string three pieces of popcorn and then three cranberries. Whatever you like, just run the needle through the berries lengthwise. You could also make a chain of just popcorn and one of just cranberries.

4. When you have finished your chain, put another small button on the end along with several knots to hold it securely.

Paper Ornaments

These simple Christmas tree decorations are easily made and quite beautiful when hung. There are designs to follow of a girl, boy, star, flower, mouse, horse, and a teapot. You can make lots of just one design or a few of each kind. They would also be fun to hang to brighten up your room on other holidays.

Here's what is needed:

white oaktag, tracing paper, carbon paper, tape
pencil, scissors, pin
black felt-tip marker, colored felt-tip markers
red embroidery floss, or string, cut into 6" lengths

Here's how to do it:

1. Place a sheet of tracing paper over the design that you would like to make.

2. Place a sheet of carbon paper over the oaktag that you will be using to make the decorations. On top of the carbon paper place the tracing paper with the design on it.

3. Gently tape at the top and bottom the three sheets together onto your working surface. This will prevent the papers from sliding around as you draw. Draw over the design on the tracing paper.

4. Remove the tracing and carbon papers. With the black fine-line felt-tip marker, draw over the designs. Cut them out. Color with the other markers.

5. With a pin, punch a hole at the top for the yarn to go through. Tie a piece of embroidery floss or string through the hole and knot it to keep it closed.

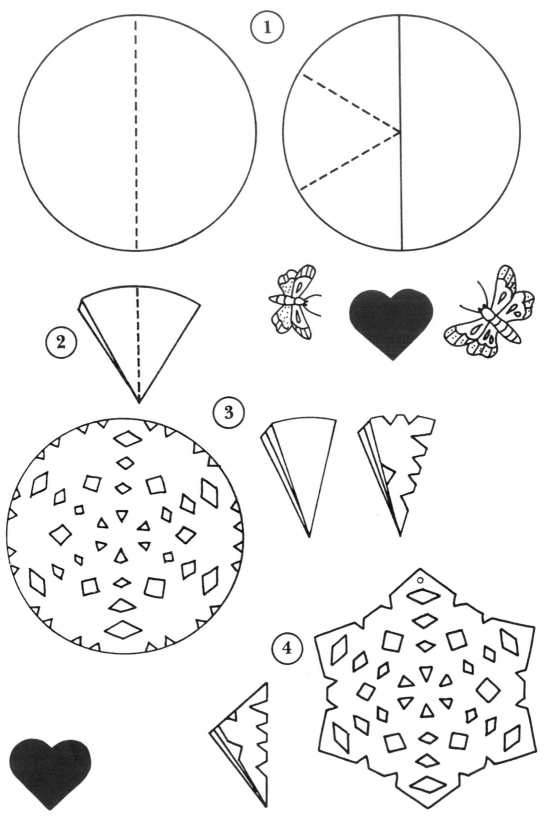

Paper Snowflakes

Snowflakes are a natural wonder, and you can make these beautiful paper ones to hang on your Christmas tree.

Here's what is needed:

white paper or construction paper
scissors, glue, cotton swabs
glass, pencil, needle, red yarn

Here's how to do it:

1. An easy way to make a beautiful snowflake is to take a circular object like a glass, and trace around it with a pencil on a piece of white paper. The bigger the circle, the bigger the snowflake you will wind up with.

2. Fold the circle in half, then in thirds, then in half again. Follow the illustrations as you go along.

3. As shown, make small cuts along the edges, but be careful not to cut away any fold completely.

4. Cut the top edge of the folded circle as the illustration shows. Be sure to make this cut on a slant. Now make another cut on this edge, as shown. With the needle, make a hole at the top of each snowflake, as shown. Cut a 6″ length of yarn for each snowflake that you make, and string the yarn through each hole.

Gingerbread Cookies ★

Gingerbread cookies have appealed to children and adults alike since the Middle Ages. During the holidays, gingerbread cookies are a very special part of the celebration and can even be hung from the Christmas tree. American colonists also enjoyed them, and it was said that George Washington's mother liked to serve them to her guests. There is a pattern for a boy and a girl cookie.

Ingredients:	**Utensils:**
⅔ cup butter, softened	large mixing bowl
½ cup sugar	mixing spoon, measuring
1 egg	cups and spoons
½ cup dark molasses	waxed paper, rolling pin
2¼ cups sifted all-purpose	lightweight cardboard,
flour	scissors
1 teaspoon baking powder	knife, cookie sheets
½ teaspoon salt	
2 teaspoons ginger	
2 teaspoons cinnamon	
½ teaspoon ground cloves	
raisins	
extra butter to grease the	
cookie sheets	

Here's how to do it:

1. Cream the butter and sugar together in the large mixing bowl. Add the egg and molasses. Continue stirring until the mixture is completely blended.

2. Add the flour, baking powder, salt, ginger, cinnamon, and cloves. Stir well; the dough will be stiff. Wrap the dough in waxed paper and chill for several hours or overnight.

3. Preheat the oven to 350°. (Ask an adult to help you do this.)

43

4. Grease the cookie sheets and then roll the dough directly onto them. Now make the pattern for the cookies out of the cardboard by first folding the cardboard lengthwise. Sketch the pattern onto the cardboard and then cut it out. Unfold it and you will have a symmetrical pattern. Grease one side of the pattern and place it on the rolled dough.

5. Now hold it in place with one hand, and cut all around the outside edge with the knife. Lift the pattern and repeat.

6. Remove the scraps of dough between the cookies. You can use these to make more cookies. Put the raisin eyes, nose, and buttons on each cookie, pressing them in gently. Place the cookie sheets in the oven and bake for 8 to 12 minutes, or until done. Makes about six large cookies.

Shortbread Cookies

These biscuit-type cakes came to America from Scotland. They have been around for three centuries and get their name from the large amount of shortening or "shortness" used in the dough.

Ingredients:

¾ cup sugar
1½ cups butter, softened
4 cups flour
extra flour to roll out the
   dough

Utensils:

large mixing bowl
mixing spoon
measuring cups
rolling pin
knife, spatula, cookie sheets

Here's how to do it:

1. Preheat the oven to 350°. (Ask an adult to help you do this.)

2. Cream the butter and sugar together thoroughly. Add one cup of flour at a time to the mixture, mixing well after each cup.

3. Spread some of the extra flour on the counter that you are going to roll the dough on. Roll the dough to a ¼" thickness. Cut into squares.

4. Using the spatula, place the cookies on ungreased cookie sheets, about an inch apart.

5. Bake for 20 minutes or until lightly browned on the edges. Makes about three dozen cookies.

Colonial Oatmeal Cookies ★

Oatmeal cookies were a popular standby in the colonial home and can still be enjoyed today. The half cup of semisweet chocolate pieces adds a nice modern touch. Chocolate was really just used in "hot chocolate" and not eaten plain or used in cooking at that time. These delicious cookies would be wonderful packed in a school lunch bag.

Ingredients:

½ cup butter
1 cup light brown sugar
1 egg, beaten
1 teaspoon vanilla
¾ cup flour
½ teaspoon salt
½ teaspoon baking powder
1½ cups instant oatmeal
1 cup of raisins
½ cup semisweet chocolate
    pieces

Utensils:

large mixing bowl
mixing spoon
measuring cups and spoons
teaspoon
cookie sheets

Here's how to do it:

1. Preheat the oven to 350°. (Ask an adult to help you do this).

2. Cream the butter, brown sugar, and egg together. Add the vanilla.

3. Add the flour, salt, and baking powder. Mix well.

4. Stir in the instant oatmeal until completely combined. Add the raisins and chocolate pieces to the batter. Mix well.

5. Drop batter from a teaspoon onto ungreased cookie sheets. Bake for 10 minutes. Makes about two dozen cookies.

Indian Slapjack ★

There are many variations of this recipe. Some are more of a pudding, but this one is for a delicious cornbread. The Indians taught the colonists all about corn, and this cornbread was made in colonial inns, bake shops, and homes.

Ingredients:

1 cup white cornmeal
1 cup all-purpose flour
1 teaspoon salt
3 teaspoons baking powder
2 tablespoons sugar
2 eggs, lightly beaten
1 cup milk
3 tablespoons butter, melted
extra butter to grease the
   pan

Utensils:

large mixing bowl
large mixing spoon
measuring cups and spoons
8″ × 8″ × 2″ pan
toothpick

Here's how to do it:

1. Preheat the oven to 350°. (Ask an adult to help you do this.)

2. Grease the pan with the extra butter.

3. In the large mixing bowl, combine the cornmeal, flour, salt, baking powder, and sugar.

4. Add the eggs, milk, and melted butter. Mix just until everything is blended.

5. Spoon the batter into the pan.

6. Bake for about 20 minutes or until a toothpick inserted into the center comes out clean. Allow to cool and then cut into pieces.

Index